T0207761

GOD
FIRST

DR. KENNETH HAROLD MCMILLAN

WESTBOW
PRESS®
A DIVISION OF THOMAS NELSON
& ZONDERVAN

WestBow Press books may be ordered through booksellers or by contacting:

WestBow Press
A Division of Thomas Nelson & Zondervan
1663 Liberty Drive
Bloomington, IN 47403
www.westbowpress.com
1 (866) 928-1240

ISBN: 978-1-9736-2916-0 (sc)
ISBN: 978-1-9736-2915-3 (e)

Library of Congress Control Number: 2018906258

Print information available on the last page.

WestBow Press rev. date: 05/30/2018

CONTENTS

PREFACE

On Thursday, October 26, 2017, the Word of the Lord came to me saying it was time to put on paper what He had communicated to me. I knew the Lord was speaking, but I was in conflict about what to do, as He was opening doors for me. I had taken several salary surveys, and my dear mother, a woman of vision, informed me about her dream, which involved me relocating to Washington, DC. I finally decided to sit still and hear from heaven. It was revealed to me that I am to write the vision God gave me, and the words to the song "I Surrender All" by CeCe Winans resonated in my spirit.

> All to Jesus I surrender
> All to Him I freely give
> I will ever love and trust Him
> In His presence daily live
> All to Jesus I surrender
> Humbly at His feet I bow
> Worldly pleasures all forsaken
> Take me, Jesus, take me now

It was not until I surrendered all that the words began to flow and my mother's dream became clearer.

I am most thankful to our Lord and Savior, Jesus Christ, for saving an old wretch, worm, and sinner like me. To feel His awesome love, one may endure combinations of pressure and love, highs and lows, and mountaintop and valley experiences. My journey has taken several years and has been full of these combinations. However, I deeply appreciate the many family members, friends, and parishioners who gave me so much love and inspiration to help bring it to fruition. Special thanks for the positive feedback from Cheryl Hitchcock, my spiritual sister and friend, who has proven to be tried and true over many years. I am especially grateful for my wife, my alter ego and better half, for being by my side throughout the experience.

Incorporating an introduction of worship in preface was key because it helped bring me into the presence of God. It also helped to organize my thoughts, release fears and anxieties, and magnify my blessings. It is my heartfelt desire to share with the world the knowledge, experience, and blessings I have attained from reading God's Word, listening to God's voice, and following His dictates. It is my belief that the sharing of life experiences and discoveries—whether good or bad—would benefit others and encourage them to change and grow in the kingdom of God. My personal prayer is that the words in this book will be food for the reader and learner, that our Lord and Savior, Jesus Christ, will be amplified and glorified, and that reading this book will be as much a joy as writing it was.

May our Lord Jesus bless you richly.

CHAPTER 1
Put God First

Matthew 6:33

When we do not put God first, there are consequences for our inaction. The result is almost always collateral damage to families and relationships. Families are torn apart because believers in the family make bad decisions about family issues. Relationships struggle and fail because one or both parties will not commit to dealing with situations in a godly manner. Inevitably, the family, personal relationships, and society suffer because people are unwilling to commit to seeking godly counsel and living according to what God has commanded. When we use the phrase "God first," we must be willing to consult the scriptures, pray, and believe that our Lord Jesus Christ will guide us in the direction that He wants us to go.

In my years of pastoring, I have discovered that the Lord really wants to be a part of our lives and guide us. Because we move so fast and make hasty decisions, the outcome is not what we desired or expected. "God first" is the starting point for any successful endeavor. If we focus on the priorities of life that

God has placed before us, He and His Word have assured us that He will handle all issues. It really boils down to a matter of trust—trusting the Word of God and believing that God will do exactly what He said He would do. We must remember that God has never lied and that He is not about to start to lie to us about our situations. "God first" is the mantra that will propel us to higher heights and deeper depths.

When we interpret what Jesus was trying to get His followers to understand, we find that it was based on obedience. God desires that we obey His Word, His darling son, Jesus, above everything. When we want both clarity and understanding about the issues of life, we must have a heartfelt desire to obey Jesus. Obedience to the Word of God is based upon trust. Trusting in and depending on the Word of God and on the Word of God alone is a sign of maturity. When we obey the Word consistently, it shows and proves to God that we are who we say we are and will to do what He commands us to do.

Interpretation of the "God first" model is important because from it we draw power and strength. It gives us a certain level of understanding that we can and should rely on the Word of God. I have learned that putting God first really simplifies my Christian walk.

The tenets of this book are interpretation, explanation, and application. As we provide an explanation for why our Lord Jesus said to "seek ye first the kingdom of God, and His righteousness" (Matthew 6:33), we must examine why we started to read the Bible for godly counsel. In this scripture, the Lord is telling us to make His priorities our priorities. To have a solid foundation in our Christian walk, we must be focused on and obedient to what the Lord tells us to do. It is about having godly order in our lives, trusting that God will direct our steps. God must reign in guidance and direction, and His will and command must be our strength and righteousness. He develops our character when He starts and finishes the work in our lives. When we seek Christ and He speaks, we should have obedience to Him and Him alone. Christ will take care of our business.

In the final phase of making sure that God is first in our lives, we must have the actual application of this model. How do we apply the idea in our everyday lives? It must be a decision of determination to walk in God's Word; we must have faith in action. For God's presence to fill our lives, we must do the things He has required of us. All through the scriptures, we see where God has required His people to be obedient to what He says. We must be willing to trust God with and at His Word. When we are confronted with troubling situations, we must have enough faith to deliver and know that God will do everything He said He would do. To apply God's Word requires a willingness to put it into action—to *do something in action and in faith.*

To develop the "God first" lifestyle, we must make sure that reading, meditating, accepting, believing, and doing God's Word are primary and central in our lives. Matthew 6:33 states, "But seek first the kingdom of God, and His righteousness; and all these things shall be added unto you." God has a perfect plan for our lives. When we do not put God first, we create a blockade. Many people say there is not enough time in a day. However, they appear to find time to handle their business or to do what they want or have planned to do. Yet they devote little to no time to God's business. God gave us twenty-four hours in a day—enough time to do what He has for us to do. The issue may be that there is not enough time to do everything He wants us to do *and* everything we want to do.

In Matthew 6:33, we are provided advice and informed of the benefits of applying it. We are advised to seek the kingdom of God and His righteousness and reminded that when we pursue the spiritual realm of God and His holiness, everything we need will be granted. It is when we do not follow the advice, as written in scripture, that we encounter barriers of many kinds. Are we willing to place God first and follow our Lord Jesus Christ?

Be obedient and follow Jesus.

CHAPTER 2

Possess Faith and Perform Works

James 2:14–26
Hebrews 11:8

In the previous chapter, we discovered that the process or idea of ensuring that God is first in everything is the absolute best way to begin the journey called life. Choosing between being able to handle our business or handle God's business must be a decision of the heart. When God is placed first, we act on moving our hands and feet, because to be motivated to change our patterns and courses, the love of Jesus Christ must be in our hearts.

> What doth it profit, my brethren, though a man say he hath faith, and have not works? can faith save him?
>
> If a brother or sister be naked, and destitute of daily food,

And one of you say unto them, Depart in peace, be ye warmed and filled; notwithstanding ye give them not those things which are needful to the body; what doth it profit?

Even so faith, if it hath not works, is dead, being alone.

Yea, a man may say, Thou hast faith, and I have works: shew me thy faith without thy works, and I will shew thee my faith by my works.

Thou believest that there is one God; thou doest well: the devils also believe, and tremble.

But wilt thou know, O vain man, that faith without works is dead?

Was not Abraham our father justified by works, when he had offered Isaac his son upon the altar?

Seest thou how faith wrought with his works, and by works was faith made perfect?

And the scripture was fulfilled which saith, Abraham believed God, and it was imputed unto him for righteousness: and he was called the Friend of God.

Ye see then how that by works a man is justified, and not by faith only.

Likewise also was not Rahab the harlot justified by works, when she had received the messengers, and had sent them out another way?

For as the body without the spirit is dead, so faith without works is dead also. (James 2:14–26)

This passage of scripture relatively explains that faith without works is dead. Jesus, our Lord, communicated this truth to James, who in turn communicated it to us. He explains that we must believe in the name of our Lord, Jesus Christ. When we believe in Christ, we experience change in our hearts, lives, and decisions. It is then that Christ takes charge of our lives.

The lordship of Jesus is paramount to being a Christian. We must follow the leadership of Jesus. Believing in Jesus and walking in faith will determine the outcome. When we place proper faith in Jesus, He will produce proper works in us. For the works to be successful, we must accept that we are no longer in control and that Jesus leads in the decision-making process in our lives. Jesus must be at the center of how we choose to conduct ourselves. The *works* part of the "faith and works" model reveals that we must be willing to walk out our faith. Walking out our faith means that we must be willing to make mistakes. When we step out on faith, we can rest assured that we will make mistakes, but we must not give up or become too weary in doing what we must do. The scripture states, "By faith Abraham, when he was called to go out into a place which he should after receive for an inheritance, obeyed; and he went out, not knowing whither he went" (Hebrews 11:8). God credited it to him as righteous because he believed God and acted in obedience. He did not just talk the talk; he walked the walk. Therefore, we refer to him as the father of our faith.

To acquire a brief interpretation of James 2:14–26, we must understand that God is illustrating that He wants to speak to us directly and expects us to be obedient to His dictates. It is easy to tell people that we are going to pray for them, as God wants us to pray. He also wants us to help when we can. It is possible, however, to enable people who are in need to be lazy. Therefore, we must be willing to ask God for a spirit of discernment so we will not become enablers. Discernment will come when we trust God enough to know that we cannot help everyone, but we will help those He sends our way. Thus, prayer and godly counsel are essential components in the lives of believers.

Many people have inundated the churches with a "using spirit." Some do not have because they have squandered what they had and simply want to use the church to acquire more. We must be careful in such encounters because people will lie to the church to get what they want. I personally believe that most blood-bought, loving Christians really want to help others; however, it has proven to be quite difficult because of the rampant scams of using spirits.

In the everyday walk and application of "faith and works," again, we must have a level of faith, believing that we must be obedient and see the world and people the way our Lord Jesus wants us to see them. Praying and meditating on God's Word daily provides the energy and strength needed to deal with people and situations. We must realize that we cannot help all, but we can help those God has placed in our path. Faith and works must become an integral part of this journey to show the world that we believe in every word in the Bible—the blueprint for life.

When we align our lives with the Word of God, we abide in it and it abides in us. When we do this, we are placing ourselves in position to ask and receive (John 15:7). We position ourselves by entering the spiritual realm of God and His holiness. Faith then takes over, and the Holy Spirit takes the lead, teaching us what to do, how to do it, and whom to help. His leadership may come via another person or as a guiding hand. It may even come in a still, small voice. It matters not how it comes, but we must be ready to act when it does. The good news is that faith is connected to works (James 2:14–26). We must have unwavering, *active* faith, and when we show our faith by our works, we are positioning ourselves to accomplish much in God's kingdom, honoring, glorifying, and lifting His name.

CHAPTER 3
Hate What God Hates

Proverbs 6:16–19
Isaiah 14:12–15
Psalm 101:7
Isaiah 59:7
2 Thessalonians 3:11
1 John 1:9

One of the surest signs of our relationship with Christ is when we can accept that Christ is truly changing our hearts. When Jesus is changing us from the inside out, we notice that we do not accept sin as we did before the great process began. Foremost, we become more aware of our own sins. During this time, we see that we need more Jesus. It is so easy to tell others about their sins and lifestyles, but when we administer a self-examination, we might not like what we find; we may, in fact, hate what we uncover. God has a unique way of showing us what is not pleasing to Him and making us hate what He hates.

Reading and meditating on God's Word is where the introspection takes place. Before we read scripture, we should ask the Holy Spirit to illuminate God's Word. By doing so, we are requesting God's guidance and direction. Guidance and direction by the Holy Spirit will lead us to understand that God desires to speak to and/or deal with us first, before we can make a fair assessment of sin that is around us. When God reveals to us what is going on with us and who we really are, conviction, by the Holy Spirit, should prompt us to change. Change requires effort and will on our part. The outcome is a strong desire to change and to become the people God wants us to be and to hate what He hates. On this Jesus journey, we must begin by staring into the depths of our own lives and at the sin that so easily ensnares us. To *hate what God hates,* we must be willing to learn from our mistakes and admit that we have not done what God wanted us to do.

Proverbs 6:16–19 states,

> These six things doth the LORD hate: yea, seven are an abomination unto him:
>
> A proud look, a lying tongue, and hands that shed innocent blood,
>
> An heart that deviseth wicked imaginations, feet that be swift in running to mischief,
>
> A false witness that speaketh lies, and he that soweth discord among brethren.

We learn that there are several things that God hates, and seven are an abomination to Him.

1. A proud look. Pride is defined as "conceit, self-love, haughtiness, and arrogance." If we possess any of these qualities, we most definitely cannot be useful in God's kingdom. This specific quality is satanic at best. There are so many scriptures that prove that God has a special disdain for this pride demon. Pride was the ultimate reason for the fall of Lucifer. Isaiah 14:12–15 states,

> How art thou fallen from heaven, O Lucifer, son of the morning! how art thou cut down to the ground, which didst weaken the nations!
>
> For thou hast said in thine heart, I will ascend into heaven, I will exalt my throne above the stars of God: I will sit also upon the mount of the congregation, in the sides of the north:
>
> I will ascend above the heights of the clouds; I will be like the most High.
>
> Yet thou shalt be brought down to hell, to the sides of the pit.

Is that why so many fall and have this spirit that is anti-God?

2. A lying tongue. A lying tongue is a language of untruths. People with a lying tongue speak untruths and know that they are doing so. It is a trick by the giver to deceive

people. God will have nothing to do with a liar; He is too holy. "He that worketh deceit shall not dwell within my house: he that telleth lies shall not tarry in my sight" (Psalm 101:7).

3. Hands that shed innocent blood. "Hands that shed innocent blood" refers to the taking of life from the harmless—people who are victims of the evils of this world and the ills of society. Their lives were taken while they were minding their own affairs. They became a collateral damage to crime, carnage, and injustice.

4. A heart that devises wicked plans. A heart that devises wicked plans is one that stores evil thoughts. People who possess such hearts tend to hurt and destroy lives and any living things that surround them. They do not wish anyone any good. They constantly think of what they can do to make the lives of others a living hades.

5. Feet that are swift to running to evil. Isaiah 59:7 states, "Their feet run to evil, and they make haste to shed innocent blood; their thoughts are thoughts of iniquity, wasting and destruction are in their paths." This means that some people cannot wait to hurt innocent people. Not only do they injure, hurt, and destroy, but they also cause tremendous damage to others all around.

6. A false witness. A false witness is an individual who gathers up false and fake reports to do harm to someone else. Oftentimes, lives and careers are destroyed because of statements made by false witnesses. They speak deceit and death.

7. One who sows discord among the brethren. Those who sow discord promote disharmony. They are referred

to as busybodies in the Bible. "For we hear that there are some which walk among you disorderly, working not at all, but are busybodies" (2 Thessalonians 3:11). Busybodies run to and from people, situations, and homes, causing strife and turmoil. They are known to tell half-truths or partial truths. Many homes and relationships have been destroyed because of the actions of such individuals.

It is not easy to interpret what God is thinking or why people continue to do things that He hates. One justifiable fact is that evil is present in this world, and foolishness seems to be winning over God's righteousness. We, as believers, must be encouraged to know that it is honorable to "hate what God hates" and to believe that the victory over sin, hatred, lies, and evil was won by the shed blood of our Lord and Savior, Jesus Christ, on the cross at Calvary. It is at the cross that we learn of ourselves and begin the process of hating what God hates. It is there that we see that the only way we can stand holy and be pleasing to God is to confess our own faults.

First John 1:9 states, "If we confess our sins, he is faithful and just to forgive us our sins, and to cleanse us from all unrighteousness." It becomes real to us, and we can apply these instructions, given to us by the Lord, in our lives. To apply God's Word on hating what God hates, we must learn to love what God loves. I have learned over the years that God loves mercy, grace, righteousness, holiness, peace, and so many other biblical virtues. A part of this process includes the fact that we must be mindful that our God is a loving God. He desires to bless and keep us conscious of the fact that some things we say and do are not pleasing to Him.

Lord Jesus, please help us to love what You love and hate what You hate. Please help us to love You and not hate! We desire so much to please You and You alone.

Much love to You, Jesus.

CHAPTER 4

Acquire the Right Temperature: Worship under the Lordship of Jesus

Revelation 3:14-22
Revelation 22:16

The church at Laodicea was a church in the New Testament that God has defined as being lukewarm. In biblical terms, *lukewarm* is not a good or pleasing term. Revelation 3:14–22 states,

> And unto the angel of the church of the Laodiceans write; These things saith the Amen, the faithful and true witness, the beginning of the creation of God;
>
> I know thy works, that thou art neither cold nor hot: I would thou wert cold or hot.

So then because thou art lukewarm, and neither cold nor hot, I will spue thee out of my mouth.

Because thou sayest, I am rich, and increased with goods, and have need of nothing; and knowest not that thou art wretched, and miserable, and poor, and blind, and naked:

I counsel thee to buy of me gold tried in the fire, that thou mayest be rich; and white raiment, that thou mayest be clothed, and that the shame of thy nakedness do not appear; and anoint thine eyes with eyesalve, that thou mayest see.

As many as I love, I rebuke and chasten: be zealous therefore, and repent.

Behold, I stand at the door, and knock: if any man hear my voice, and open the door, I will come in to him, and will sup with him, and he with me.

To him that overcometh will I grant to sit with me in my throne, even as I also overcame, and am set down with my Father in his throne.

He that hath an ear, let him hear what the Spirit saith unto the churches.

The church at Laodicea was defined as being self-satisfying. The members attempted to have and do church the way that they wanted. They were not interested in doing the things that God wanted them to do. In fact, it was more a spirit of doing things partially and half-heartedly. When we bear the name of Jesus Christ, we must be purposeful in recognizing that He is head of His church. Jesus gives the church its course of direction. When we belong to Him, He is Master and Lord. The lordship of Jesus is the only way a church can be successful. The love of Jesus must be present at all stations and in all ministries of the church. The church at Laodicea had a righteousness of its own. There was a strong presence of doing ministry their own way. It is almost as though this church was self-sufficient and not in need of Jesus or His ways.

Spiritual vision is necessary and needed in any church that bears or wears the name of Jesus. The church must have the heart and mind of Jesus. The church at Laodicea depended more on its riches and money than it did on Christ and His Holy Spirit. When money, wealth, and riches are the primary focal point of any church, the body is headed for trouble. The love of Jesus and His love for His people are the foundational principles in the Bible-teaching and Bible-believing church where I serve as pastor. When a church begins to rely more on its wealth and riches, it becomes very worldly. It becomes a place of self-deception where the members believe more in the dollar bill than they do in Jesus. It is a sad scenario when God has tasked the church to do business for Him and the members decide to do their own business. We all want to handle business for our Lord, Jesus Christ, but we must be willing to put the ideals of this world behind us. We must claim a new value system, a system that is based upon the biblical and the heavenly, and not a system that is based upon the world and what it values. In Revelation 22:16a, Jesus Himself states, "I Jesus have sent mine angel to testify unto you these things in the churches."

When the Lord speaks to His church and her people, they must be willing to listen. When He leads the church to stop doing a certain thing, the church must stop. The church is also admonished to start doing the things that He wants us to do; we do not have a choice in the matter in terms of direction. We (the church) must follow Jesus at all costs. If Jesus refers to us or to the church as being *lukewarm,* it is not a compliment. It is a loving God telling us that we must change our wicked ways. When Christ gives counsel, we must have a mind-set to do what He has called us to do—repent. In repentance, we must confess to our Lord Jesus that we have not lived up to His dictates. We must be willing and ready to change; it is never easy in our own strength. When Christ is present in us, the Holy Spirit will convict. Conviction means it is time for a positive change. We must look to Jesus to set us on the course of being right with Him again. We must look to obedience and ask God for counsel. We must then look to the heart to move us in faith.

Again, being lukewarm is not a good place. Jesus makes it abundantly clear that He desires for us to be *hot.* We must have a zest and zeal to please Him and Him alone. Why is this important? Because when we understand that God has a master plan, we can ask Him to share it with us. God does not share a lot with us until we prove and show Him that we are trustworthy. Getting an understanding of what God is saying is important. When we understand that God desires for us to crucify more of our wills and wants, then we can become more pleasing to Him.

Jesus desires that we have a heart for His people and the issues that challenge them. People are permitted to wander in darkness for a while, but we are duty-bound to go to where they are and bring them to Christ. Being lukewarm causes us to only care about what is important to us. We should make a concerted effort to die to self and grab more of Jesus.

The instructions that Jesus gives include direction to be zealous (all out, all in) and repent (stop, turn, change, confess). The people and the church must be willing to acknowledge that they have made mistakes and that they desire to change. When Christ speaks and we recognize His voice, we must be willing to move. He was telling the church at Laodicea that He desired to fellowship more with them. He wanted them to receive His holy and divine directives.

God has a special and unique blessing for those who are willing to receive His rebuke. Getting us on the right track is what God desires. When we are "hot" for Jesus, our light will shine. We will be salt and make a difference in this world. We cannot be stopped or hidden.

In summary, the church, the body of Christ, must be on fire for God. After all, it is the church that God left on earth as a model. In Revelation 3:14–22, God expresses His desire for the church on a spiritual level. The church in this scripture is much like many churches of today. Some members who make up the body in some churches appear to have it made in the shade. They talk and act as if they have everything and need nothing. In this state, they are useless to God because He wants us to be dependent on Him—not on ourselves. He also wants our focus to be on Him and not on possessions of this world. He wants us to enjoy them but not let them take His place. In Revelation 3:18, He gives the church at Laodicea directives on what to do in order to see what they need to see, to do what they need to do. The same message is for the church today.

Revelation 3:21a states, "To him that overcometh will I grant to sit with me in my throne." Thus, the saints will be exalted when we prevail in the spirit of obedience. It is a beautiful sight when we acknowledge that God has allowed us to be used by Him, despite our shortcomings.

Thank You so much, Lord Jesus, for being the God of a second chance.

Thank You, and much love.

CHAPTER 5
Test and Try God with Promise

Malachi 3:2; 3:3
Malachi 3:8–10
Psalm 17:3; 68:9
Proverbs 8:21
Matthew 6:33; 14:20

The book of Malachi represents the close of the Old Testament prophets. His message gave a warning and admonition for the people to prepare themselves for a new work that the Lord was about to do. A careful examination of the book and the prophet reveals that God has treasures that He would like for us to possess. When we question whether we can handle God's business, we should consider the graphic picture of the closing of the Old Testament history. It portrays great reforms that were needed to prepare the way for the coming Messiah. The writer intends for us to know that God wants His people to return to Him. Specifically, humankind had moved so far away from God and His desires for them. It is a similar picture of what is going on in modern society. People are more self-absorbed today than in previous times. Mankind has always been selfish, but the atmosphere today is more defined by "selfies" and selfishness.

In the book of Malachi, again it is evident the writer has a style and form of being forceful but personal. God—Jehovah God—is represented as having a conversation with His dear people. The writer uses the phrase "You say" often. It is contrasted with some of the other Old Testament writers who used the phrase "Thus says the Lord." I do believe that God was preparing His people for a new work and a fresh anointing that was about to come forth. When God speaks to us now, He uses the words of Jesus in the New Testament. To develop the idea of being the concealment of Christ in the Old Testament, we must look at it through the prism of *trust*—trusting God before any other process is required. We must remember that faith and trust are synonyms.

Handling God's business must mean that we are willing to say that God is right and we are wrong. Our ways of thinking and doing must be modified and changed. Modification, like sanctification, is a process in time in which God separates us and readies us for service back to Him. Malachi uses the analogy of a "refiner's fire" in Malachi 3:2. He also states, in Malachi 3:3, "And he shall sit as a refiner and purifier of silver: and he shall purify the sons of Levi, and purge them as gold and silver, that they may offer unto the LORD an offering in righteousness." Our lives must be tested by the fire and trials of life. When we show and demonstrate that we can be trusted, we develop a spirit of faithfulness in the eyes of God. Remember, when we show God evidence that He wants and deserves, we know that God is doing a work in us that He alone can do.

The "inward life" must be tried. Psalm 17:3 states, "Thou hast proved mine heart; thou hast visited me in the night; thou hast tried me, and shalt find nothing; I am purposed that my mouth shall not transgress." There must be changes that God performs on us in the inside of our hearts. We must be willing vessels. There are sacrifices that we must make for God to trust us.

Malachi 3:8–10 states,

> Will a man rob God? Yet ye have robbed me. But ye say, Wherein have we robbed thee? In tithes and offerings.
>
> Ye are cursed with a curse: for ye have robbed me, even this whole nation.
>
> Bring ye all the tithes into the storehouse, that there may be meat in mine house, and prove me now herewith, saith the LORD of hosts, if I will not open you the windows of heaven, and pour you out a blessing, that there shall not be room enough to receive it.

In this passage, one simple question is asked: "Will a man rob God?" The answer to the question is yes. For us to understand this question, we need to remember that God believes that some or most of His people have given their all. There was a spirit of disobedience and self- righteousness that hindered them. Self-righteousness is any attempt to meet God's standards based upon one's own merits. We have a definition of what to do that is not based upon what God has called and required us to do. Again, God is conveying the message that we must change our ways of thinking and doing and understand that He is right and we are wrong. To handle our business, we must know what God says and what He requires; then we must handle His business first.

How does this apply to us? How are we supposed to continue and function? We must read the entire Bible and trust the promises of God. The Lord says that if we do this His way and not our way, we can be assured of His favor and blessings. The opposite is true if we do not do what God tells us to do. He says that we will be "cursed with a curse" (Malachi 3:9). It is all predicated on the fact that we have robbed God by not using our talents, treasures, and/or time serving Him. Money and finances are one way in which one can tell if believers are who they say they are. When we hold onto the tithe and justify it by our own merits, we are telling God that we really do not trust Him. It is as if we are saying to God, "I have other things to do with my money. I will or might take care of You later."

Being busy is another way of not giving back to God. The acronym BUSY stands for Being under Satan's Yoke. I do not know how biblical that is, but I see it to be true in many instances. The state of always being busy means that we have not made God a priority. Remember chapter 1: "God *first*."

We need to understand that we would make progress if we would only trust God and His Word. The dictates and promises of God are stated in Malachi 3:10: "'Bring ye all the tithes into the storehouse, that there may be meat in mine house, and prove me now herewith,' saith the LORD of hosts, 'if I will not open you the windows of heaven, and pour you out a blessing, that there shall not be room enough to receive it.'" It is written that we are required to bring all our tithes to His storehouse (the local church), and when we are obedient to this command, God promises the following:

1. Spiritual showers. Psalm 68:9 states, "Thou, O God, didst send a plentiful rain, whereby thou didst confirm thine inheritance, when it was weary."

2. Windows of heaven opened. Floodgates of the sky represent the superabundance of God.

3. Spiritual fullness. Our deepest needs will be satisfied. Proverbs 8:21 states, "That I may cause those that love me to inherit substance; and I will fill their treasures."

4. Blessings. God's favor and protection—temporal and spiritual. Matthew 6:33 states, "But seek ye first the kingdom of God, and his righteousness; and all these things shall be added unto you."

5. Superabundance. Having more than enough. "There will not be room enough to receive it" (Malachi 3:10). The wow factor is evident; it is God's provision as indicated in Matthew 14:20: "And they did all eat, and were filled: and they took up of the fragments that remained." God is showing and proving to us repeatedly that He can, will, and should be trusted. For us to test and try God, we must be willing to read, study, and trust God's Word. Doing so is a major step in handling God's business.

CHAPTER 6

Praise/Trust/Obey/Reap

Psalm 22:3–5
Psalm 37
Proverbs 4:12–14
John 8:29

The book of Psalms reveals that God has a special way of speaking to His people—in the form of songs. We should understand that when we sing songs or Psalms to God, He is well pleased. God's holiness is evident when we praise Him for who He is. Psalm 22:3–5 states,

> But thou art holy, O thou that inhabitest the praises of Israel.
>
> Our fathers trusted in thee: they trusted, and thou didst deliver them.
>
> They cried unto thee, and were delivered: they trusted in thee, and were not confounded.

To handle God's business, we must be willing to meet Him in praise. Our praises should give Him honor and glory. We should not always ask God for blessings. As His people, we should desire to be in His company and presence because that is the desire of our hearts. The principle addressed in this book regarding the management of God's business is centered around trusting God and His Word. Without unequivocally trusting God, we will not be able to establish a firm foundational relationship. Confidence in God and in His Word is the key and central theme of praising Him in the entire book of Psalms.

In Psalm 37, King David writes about the heritage of the righteous and the calamity of the wicked. I personally believe that we can possess the belief and value system David noted in Psalm 37. We, too, can regroup and regain God's trust and confidence. In Psalm 37, David encourages believers to live a life that models love for God. He also encourages believers to trust in God and His ways and reap the benefits of divine protection. The prominent theme of Psalm 37 is centered around promises to all believers.

The issue of handling God's business above and before our business is prevalent in Psalm 37:1–2. David states, "Fret not thyself because of evildoers, neither be thou envious against the workers of iniquity. For they shall soon be cut down like the grass, and wither as the green herb." God makes it abundantly clear that the wicked will be cut off. The ungodly, sinful people will be dealt with by God Himself. When we contrast the righteous with the wicked, we observe that God makes a distinction between saints and sinners. The end or fate of the wicked is punishment and separation from God. God places penalties on His people for willful disobedience. He desires His people to be a model of who He is. We are called to make a difference for our Lord and Savior, Jesus Christ. In Psalm 37, God says that they (the wicked) are snared by their own evil acts and the acts of others. If we are more concerned about how others are living than about living a purposeful and meaningful life for Jesus, our fate will be just as theirs.

Psalm 37:3–10 states,

> Trust in the LORD, and do good; so shalt thou dwell in the land, and verily thou shalt be fed.

> Delight thyself also in the LORD: and he shall give thee the desires of thine heart.

> Commit thy way unto the LORD; trust also in him; and he shall bring it to pass.

> And he shall bring forth thy righteousness as the light, and thy judgment as the noonday.

> Rest in the LORD, and wait patiently for him: fret not thyself because of him who prospereth in his way, because of the man who bringeth wicked devices to pass.

> Cease from anger, and forsake wrath: fret not thyself in any wise to do evil.

> For evildoers shall be cut off: but those that wait upon the LORD, they shall inherit the earth.

> For yet a little while, and the wicked shall not be: yea, thou shalt diligently consider his place, and it shall not be.

In the major core of the psalm, verbs such as *trust, dwell, delight, commit, rest,* and *cease* (from anger) are used. The verbs represent the action that we must take and make on our journeys into pleasing God. Our firmest and strongest desire must be to believe in the unadulterated Word of God, trusting God at His Word and living a life that proves and honors Him. There is an earthly heritance in verse 11: "But the meek shall inherit the earth, and shall delight themselves in the abundance of peace." It is our aim to please God and demonstrate that we have total faith and trust in Him. In Psalm 37:23–24, David states, "The steps of a good man are ordered by the LORD: and he delighteth in his way. Though he fall, he shall not be utterly cast down: for the LORD upholdeth him with his hand."

So many of us have fallen because of disobedience—not following the dictates of the Holy Spirit and/or not completing tasks assigned by the Lord. However, the Lord intervened and held us up. It is obvious that God requires total faith, trust, and obedience.

When the Lord orders our steps, we will go where He wants us to go and when He tells us to go. When God orders our steps, we will communicate with people we may not or would not ordinarily communicate with. The ordering of the saints' steps is a picture of God's divine guidance. With divine guidance comes divine favor and divine support. Solomon states in Proverbs 4:12–14,

> When thou goest, thy steps shall not be straitened; and when thou runnest, thou shalt not stumble.

> Take fast hold of instruction; let her not go: keep her; for she is thy life.

> Enter not into the path of the wicked, and go not in the way of evil men.

Divine guidance occurs when we have a personal and true relationship with Jesus. When He speaks, we listen and move. There should not be any stalling or making excuses. Movement of the feet is necessary. Divine favor is when you know that that God gives you spiritual (personal) blessings because you choose to heed His voice. Divine favor is promised to the obedient saints, and it is possessed by our desire to please God and not humans. It is a characteristic of Christ. Matthew 3:17 states, "And lo a voice from heaven, saying, 'This is my beloved Son, in whom I am well pleased.'" John 8:29 states, "And he that sent me is with me: the Father hath not left me alone; for I do always those things that please him." It should be our Christian duty to walk pleasingly in the precepts of our Lord and Savior, Jesus Christ.

One of my favorite verses in all scripture is Psalm 37:25: "I have been young, and now am old; yet have I not seen the righteous forsaken, nor his seed begging bread." This is the absolute truth—we are assured that if we obey the Word of God and honor Jesus, we will experience the goodness and glory of God. If we handle God's business and trust that He handles ours, we are setting ourselves up for His blessings.

Applying and putting this in perspective, we can see that our God is a good, trustworthy, and faithful God. He has proven Himself and promised us blessings upon blessings if we would only trust Him. When we trust and obey God, the biblical truth is that God will take care of us: "The wicked watcheth the righteous, and seeketh to slay him. The LORD will not leave him in his hand, nor condemn him when he is judged" (Psalm 37:32–33). God has assured us in this division of the psalm that He will give us divine protection from on high. Be encouraged to start the process of receiving your biblical heritage from the Lord and walk in His ways.

CHAPTER 7

Seek God: The Duty of All People

Philippians 1:3-6
Isaiah 40:31
Jeremiah 20:96

Regarding personal evaluation, when we, as believers, have walked in the plan that God has for our lives, we can be assured that fruit will be produced. In evaluating or assessing ourselves, we should look inwardly and ask several questions: "Am I living a productive life? Did I allow and accept God's plan of sanctification? Did I do the things God wanted me to do?"

The writer records in Philippians 1:3-6,

> I thank my God upon every remembrance of you,
>
> Always in every prayer of mine for you all making request with joy,

> For your fellowship in the gospel from the first day until now;
>
> Being confident of this very thing, that he which hath begun a good work in you will perform it until the day of Jesus Christ.

This is a model prayer for the church and the saints who comprise the church. God's work will be completed. We should ask ourselves, "Did I do my part? Was I an active participant in the lives of others that God placed in my path?" Our Lord Jesus believes that our answer should be unequivocally "Yes, Lord Jesus." When our prayer lives are in direct communication with God, we should be listening first and then responding with "Yes, Lord Jesus, I will." God has given us an opportunity to speak directly with Him to determine our next moves. Sometimes God wants us to stop; at other times, He wants us to wait or step out on faith.

When we move, we must accept the fact that there may be some pitfalls, battles, confrontations, and tribulations. With the bumps and bruises, we must, however, be obedient to the voice of Jesus. When we realize that God's desire is that we wait, we must stand strong until we receive His instructions as to when to move. Remaining in place and waiting on the Lord has blessings and favor attached. Isaiah 40:31 states, "But they that wait upon the LORD shall renew their strength; they shall mount up with wings as eagles; they shall run, and not be weary; and they shall walk, and not faint." This is proof that waiting on the Lord has spiritual power and that our spirits are renewed as a result. Waiting on the Lord to tell us when to go or stay will increase our prayer lives. It will also equip us with a deeper and better understanding of what it is like to have a personal relationship with Jesus. Ultimately, God shows us that His strength is promised. To be successful and have peace in our lives, we must have moral and spiritual strength that can only come from Jesus. When the Lord strengthens us via the Holy Spirit or His Word, then and only then can we be life- and world-changers—salt and light.

Inaction, or the refusal to move, can have dire consequences for the believer who does not move when the Lord says to move. When we make a comparison and contrast of *action* and *inaction,* the result is two different perspectives. My personal belief is that inaction cannot be an option. Life will happen, whether we take the gospel to the world or not. For this world to be a better place and for lives to be changed, we must be active participants with whomever and wherever the Lord assigns us. We must make godly decisions about how to run the Christian race and live holy, obedient, and results-oriented lives. When we accept the fact that God truly desires to use us, we will be positioning ourselves for lives of purpose. We will set priorities, make sacrifices, and attain results.

Priorities

Priorities are facts or conditions that are regarded and treated as more important—things that are regarded as important and first. As we understand from the "God first" model, God has given us simple, clear, Holy Spirit-filled directives and instructions on how to move and have our being. When our primary focus and purpose in life is to be pleasing unto Jesus, we must have the mental and spiritual mind-set of doing God's will. I personally believe, without any doubt, that true believers will endure to the end. Faith and belief in the lordship of Jesus must be our guiding light. When we have been washed by the blood of the Lamb and have accepted Christ, He will separate and sanctify us. We will be like Jeremiah—the Holy Spirit in us will be "like fire shut up in our bones" (Jeremiah 20:9). When we accept the gift of Jesus and His Holy Spirit, we believe wholeheartedly that we will never fall away from God's great gift of grace. I teach perseverance of the saints—that God's grace is sufficient to keep us in all situations if we just keep hold of His unchanging hand. "Jesus, we know that you have us."

Sacrifices

The term *sacrifice* is defined as a loss, or something one gives up—usually for the sake of a better cause. Sacrifices are linked to consecration, devotion, dedication, and commitment. These terms describe God's perfect model—how we should look in Jesus. Our Lord gave a perfect illustration of sacrifice, devotion, dedication, and commitment. He gave the ultimate in sacrifices by dying on an old, rugged cross for us—love and sacrifice. Thus, loving God, committing to please Jesus, and making sacrifices must be our primary goals. This is, in essence, handling God's business first, while trusting Him to take care of our personal business—our needs and desires.

Results

The term *results* is defined as consequences, effects, or outcomes. I have decided that I must conduct a personal reassessment to determine if my life is pleasing to God. We should desire to have lives where God can use us to make a difference in His kingdom and with His people. We should ask, "Is my Lord and Savior, Jesus Christ, pleased with where I am in life? Am I ready to seek personal and attainable goals from the Lord? Am I willing to commit to a deeper, more disciplined prayer life?" When we ask ourselves these difficult questions, we must believe that our Lord will give us the answers that we need. We must ask for help and guidance from the Holy Spirit. God's Spirit will convict us in the areas that stand out as being out of order. We serve a loving and awesome God who is so very ready to use us. We are needed in the kingdom. When we step out on faith, we leave the success and results to a holy God. God's desire for us is to have faith and trust in Him. He has never let His children go without His comfort and presence. Let's trust God with every aspect of our lives.

CHAPTER 8
Finish Well

Matthew 25
Hebrews 11:6
Philippians 4:13
Romans 10:9–13
1Timothy 1:12

Well done, thy good and faithful servant. I believe these are some of the greatest words in all scripture. To hear our Creator say "well done" is the most prized of all possessions. Our number one goal in this life should be to hear the voice of Jesus say, "Well done." I imagine seeing Jesus face-to-face and the joy of being in His presence. The term *overwhelmed* is an understatement; I am not sure if there are human terms to describe this emotion. My perception is that of faithfully working in the kingdom. Can we fathom that one day the God of the universe will praise us for the work that we did for Him? Can we fathom that one day God Almighty—all by Himself— will give us a commendation of thanks for our faithful service? Can we fathom that He sees that we have decided to invest all we have—all He has given us—into His plan and program during our lifetimes? Can we fathom that one day we will have lived the creed that He has set before us? Matthew 25:23 is an encouragement for us to keep going and to ensure we do not acquire an attitude of quitting or giving up: "His lord said unto him, Well done, good and faithful servant; thou hast been faithful over a few things, I will make thee ruler over many things: enter thou into the joy of thy lord."

God does not use the word *if,* and *if* is not a part of the conversation that we will have with our Lord. God wants us to be engaged in soul-winning—leading the unsaved to Christ—and in lives being changed. To hear the Master say "well done" is the prize of prizes. We must never lose sight of the fact that Jesus has already won the war; we must live lives in which we are willing to take Him with us into every battle.

In Matthew 25:21–25, our Lord is commending His servant for being faithful to the master. The word *stewardship* means obligation and duty to one's master. The dictionary definition of stewardship is the "conducting, supervising, or managing of something; especially the careful and responsible management of something entrusted in one's care." When we express consideration for the well-being of God's people and God's property, a promised reward and blessing await us. When the Lord allows us to take care of His people, handle His business, and seek His direction, we realize that we can be good stewards if we trust Him totally and explicitly.

Hebrews 11:6 states, "But without faith it is impossible to please Him, for he who cometh to God must believe that He is, and that he is a rewarder of them that diligently seek Him." God gives promises to those who seek Him with a sincere heart and establishes nonnegotiable requirements. It is a matter of faith and obedience. Remember the model of "faith and works." Our faith must be accompanied by our works. Because we believe, we do (respond); we become obedient stewards and servants of Jesus. Doing and serving in obedience to Christ increases our personal faith. I have noticed that in some areas of our lives, or in difficult circumstances, we may deal with a spirit of unbelief. When we get to this place, we must remind ourselves of the state of this Christian journey. The "God first" model must come back into play when we look back and review the fact that our only desire is to please God. To hear the words "well done," we must be willing to slow down and have a conversation with Jesus by becoming readers, hearers, and doers of the holy Word. To encourage ourselves, we must be willing to have deeper, dedicated prayer lives that include asking God to speak to us and telling Him we are listening.

When we put God first in our decisions, we can expect God to produce the outcome. Staying focused on making decisions that are pleasing to God should be our aim and focus. The plan to which we must adhere includes goal-setting and godly aspirations—God's goals, not our own. My personal desire to please God has been a major goal and focal point in my life. Goals set by God should be the driving force to accomplish one's plan. Unattainable goals are worthless. We must have goals that line up with the voice of Jesus and His holy Word. Some of our goals will require effort and sacrifices. We should ask ourselves, "Am I willing to make the necessary sacrifices? Am I willing to give His projects my full attention and the effort that is required?" Our response should be a resounding yes and "Yes, Lord, yes."

We are the body of Christ, in need of assistance on this Christian journey. Some of our goals include seeking assistance from others in our quest to seek and achieve godly goals and aspirations. When we bring our common goals together, we see that Jesus is magnified and glorified in all the earth. We must challenge ourselves to go deeper, to meditate more, to encourage one another, and above all, to pray and seek God's face daily. *Well* and *done* are the words that Christ will give to all who believe and trust in Him and work in His kingdom, as there is no other way to God except through Jesus. Romans 10:9–13 states,

> That if thou shalt confess with thy mouth the Lord Jesus, and shalt believe in thine heart that God hath raised him from the dead, thou shalt be saved.

> For with the heart man believeth unto righteousness; and with the mouth confession is made unto salvation.

> For the scripture saith, Whosoever believeth on him shall not be ashamed.

> For there is no difference between the Jew and the Greek: for the same Lord over all is rich unto all that call upon him.

> For whosoever shall call upon the name of the Lord shall be saved.

This passage of scripture makes it abundantly clear that this journey is going to be worth all the joy and compensation, laughter and tears, smiles and frowns. We must be encouraged to go out and believe that our Lord Jesus has called us to be agents of change in this world. Our faith can take us to higher heights and deeper depths than our finite minds can imagine.

In closing, consider Philippians 4:13: "I can do all things through Christ which strengtheneth me." This is a good example of enabling grace. Grace is the free and unmerited favor or beneficence of God. It is God's kindness and favor. The world should see the kindness of Jesus displayed through our lives, actions, and deeds. When God grants us favor to do His inviting and to handle His business, it should be a badge of honor for the humble servants whose personal desire is to hear Jesus say, "Well done my good and faithful servant; well done." I, like Paul, in imparting an encouraging word to Timothy, his young protégé and partner, states, "And I thank Christ Jesus our Lord, who hath enabled me, for that he counted me faithful, putting me into the ministry" (1 Timothy 1:12). I pray that our Lord Jesus richly blesses you as you travel this Jesus journey, putting God *first*.

Until He returns, much love.

God's Business   *My Business*

God's business always outweighs my business.
His business is top priority!

ABOUT THE AUTHOR

Dr. Kenneth Harold McMillan is the pastor of the Link Baptist Church, a contemporary and multicultural house of worship. With great passion and love for the Lord, he teaches the Word of God with biblical and practical integrity, with balance, and *without* compromise. In *God First*, he outlines several principles we must follow to be truly blessed and to earn the commendation, "Well done, thou good and faithful servant."

Printed in the United States
By Bookmasters